# Norman Bethune

### Roderick Stewart

Fitzhenry & Whiteside Limited

# Contents

**THE CANADIANS**
*A Continuing Series*

## Norman Bethune
*Author:* Roderick Stewart
*Design:* Jack Steiner
*Cover Illustration:* John Mardon

Fitzhenry & Whiteside acknowledge with thanks the Canada Council for the Arts, the Government of Canada through its Book Publishing Industry Development Program, and the Ontario Arts Council for their support of our publishingh program.
**National Library of Canada Cataloguing in Publication**
Stewart, Roderick, 1934–
Norman Bethune / Roderick Stewart. — 2nd ed.
(Canadians)
Includes bibliographical references and index.
ISBN 1-55041-487-9
1. Bethune, Norman, 1890–1939. 2. Surgeons—Canada—Biography.
3. Surgeons—China—Biography. I. Title. II. Series.

R464.B4S75 2002          617'.092          C00-930542-4

© 2002 Fitzhenry & Whiteside Limited
195 Allstate Parkway, Markham, Ontario L3R 4T8

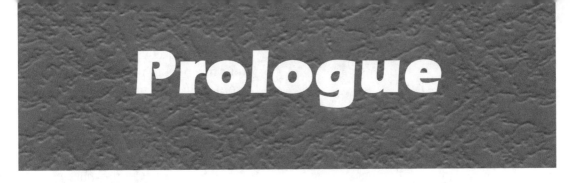

# Prologue

## Saranac Lake, New York

A few final brush strokes and the artist steps back to survey his work. Dominating the painting is an angel, who holds in his arms the frail, lifeless body of a small child. Near him is a church, and beyond in the graveyard, are several tombstones, one of which reads, "Norman Bethune. Died 1932."

*At Trudeau Sanatorium, Saranac Lake, New York, 1927*

Beneath the kneeling angel is a verse:

*Sweet death, thou kindest angel of them all,*
*Into thy soft arms at last, O let me fall,*
*Bright stars are out, gone the burning sun,*
*My little act is over, the tiresome play is done.*

For a long moment he hesitates, then moves forward to sign his name, "Norman Bethune, October 1927."

Suffering from tuberculosis, he had been a sanatorium patient for nearly a year. As his condition worsened, he was on the point of giving up his struggle. In desperation, rather than wait any longer while the terrible disease slowly ate away his lungs, he worked out a plan for taking his own life. He explained it to his fellow patients: after rowing to the centre of the nearby lake, he would inject himself with morphine, slip into the water and begin to swim. Death, he assured them, would come quickly and painlessly.

Fortunately, he did not carry out his morbid plan; nor did death come when he predicted. Instead, his health improved dramatically. Within weeks, his surprised doctors agreed that he was well enough to leave the sanatorium.

This release from what he had believed to be certain death increased his energies and redirected his talents. From that point he set off on a path that though sometimes lonely and uncomfortable, and often dangerous, led to adventures and achievements that would make him an international hero.

# Chapter 1
# Ontario and Europe

*The restored Manse in Gravenhurst, Ontario*

Norman Bethune was born on March 3, 1890, in the booming Ontario lumber town of Gravenhurst in the Muskoka Lakes district, one hundred and fifty kilometres north of Toronto. His father, the Reverend Malcolm Nicolson Bethune, and his mother, Elizabeth Ann had moved into the Presbyterian manse on John Street in June, 1889. Malcolm, who had just entered the ministry, had gone to Gravenhurst to preach in his first church.

When Norman was only three years old, the family left Gravenhurst for Beaverton, where Reverend Bethune preached for four years. From there they moved to Toronto for two years, then to Aylmer, back to Toronto, on to Blind River, next to Sault Ste. Marie, and finally to Owen Sound, where Norman finished high school at the age of seventeen. By moving so often from church to church, Norman's father made it impossible for the Bethune family to plant roots deeply in the soil of any community. Throughout his life Norman would be a restless adventurer. His inability to stay long in one place was most likely linked to this childhood experience.

Most of the places where Norman lived as a boy were small towns located near Ontario woods and lakes. In those early years the thrill of roaming freely in the forests or along the shores of Georgian Bay and Lake Superior kindled in him an intense love of the outdoors, a passion he never lost. Taking easily to individual sports, he became a strong swimmer, a good skater, and an expert log-roller. As a result, he developed a lean, muscular physique: broad shoulders, powerful arms and a strikingly erect posture.

He also had a perceptive, penetrating mind that acted and reacted quickly. Aware at an early age of his abilities, he was a

*Norman aged 9, Janet, his sister, and Malcolm, his brother*

*At age 15 in Owen Sound*

self-confident, bold and daring child who was fiercely determined to think and act for himself.

During the family's first stay in Toronto when he was only six years old, he walked out of the house one morning. By early evening, after several searches of the neighbourhood had failed to locate him, his worried parents called the police. At twilight, he strolled into the kitchen and casually announced that he had just walked all the way across Toronto, a distance of almost fifteen kilometres. Surprised at his parents' concern and irritated by their anger, he hungrily ate his supper while his father scolded him, and went up to bed thoroughly pleased with his day's exploration.

He also learned quickly to stand up for his rights. At a rented summer cottage, the landlord refused to let the Bethune children play on the lawn unless their father paid a higher rent. Norman stormed into the house to protest that this was unfair. He became angry, not only with the landlord for being unjust, but also with his father for failing to protest against the injustice.

It was never easy to manage Norman. Though Malcolm and Elizabeth were strict with their son, it required all their endurance and skill to harness a curious, impatient and self-willed boy who wanted to sample all the pleasures of life, including the forbidden. Despite their inability to control him, they did succeed in convincing him of the need to serve others, especially the unfortunate and the underprivileged. And so he grew up with a dual nature: one side of him yearned for adventure and luxury and the other demanded discipline and service. These contradictory impulses would remain with him forever, leading him on the zigzag path that became his life.

Norman graduated with honours from Owen Sound Collegiate in June, 1907, but instead of following some of his classmates to university, he spent the following year working as a lumberjack north of Lake Superior. When the job ended, he returned home near Christmas to teach in a one-room schoolhouse in the hamlet of Edgely just north of Toronto. He began by making it clear to his pupils that he was in charge. On his first day in the school he laid down a set of rules on behaviour. Not at all ready to accept their new schoolmaster's discipline, a few of the boys, who were almost as old as Bethune, decided to test him. Bethune met their challenge by punishing those who broke his rules. When even his use of the strap failed to impress one pupil, Bethune expelled him. The following morning he found the word "spittoon" splashed in fresh paint on the school fence. A few days later, some of the boys brought in a local bully to rough up their teacher.

He was waiting as Bethune left the school late one afternoon. Taller by a head than Bethune, he was broad shouldered and heavy set. As Bethune opened the gate, the young man stepped up to him and said in a baiting tone, "The boys tell me you're real handy with the strap. Let's see how you are with your fists." Then he lunged forward and swung at Bethune, who dodged the blow. Throwing his books aside, he ducked the next punch too, then swung himself, catching the attacker squarely on the jaw. As his opponent staggered, Bethune charged at him, landing blow after blow on the bigger man, who tumbled to the ground.

Bethune stood over him, ready to carry on the fight, but his opponent cringed. Holding up his hands to protect his face he cried, "No more! I've had enough!"

Scooping up his hat, the attacker scrambled to his feet and ran off down the street.

*With fellow workers at Frontier College, 1912. The Reverend Alfred Fitzpatrick is third from the right.*

This decisive contest, which was witnessed by a group of boys hiding behind the school, brought an abrupt end to Bethune's discipline problems at Edgely school.

In the autumn of 1909, he entered a science course at University College, University of Toronto, where he spent the next two years. By then, bored and looking for a change, he let his wandering mind lead him back to the northern woods. What attracted him was a new and unusual school called Frontier College. The school's director, Reverend Alfred Fitzpatrick, had explained to Bethune how it operated. In return for free room and board, instructors spent their evenings teaching immigrant working men the English language and Canadian history. During the day they worked with their students laying railway tracks, building bridges or hauling logs.

After listening to Mr. Fitzpatrick's description of the work, Bethune immediately volunteered. By day he was an axeman. By night he ran the reading room in the logging camp on the north shore of Georgian Bay. He loved the life, a combination of hard physical work in the Canadian outdoors, and service to others. On New Year's Eve, as the other men gathered to celebrate the holiday, Bethune set the broken leg of a lumberjack and hauled him by sleigh to the railroad, where he could be taken to hospital in Sudbury.

Collecting his pay the following spring, he took a fun-filled holiday jaunt in the American mid-west that landed him broke and jobless in Winnipeg. There he worked for several weeks as a reporter with a Winnipeg newspaper before returning to Toronto.

In September, ready to settle down again, he entered the Faculty of Medicine at the University of Toronto. For the next two years he did well academically. He studied, attended most classes, and turned in assignments on time. The result was good marks in all his courses except for French and German, which he found difficult. His inability to learn foreign languages was a weakness that would remain with him throughout his life.

The summer of 1914 passed quickly and quietly for Bethune as he prepared to enter his third year of medical school. Then, with the autumn term a few weeks away, he made a dramatic change in his plans. On August 4, Great Britain declared war on Germany. As a colony of Great Britain,

Canada was automatically involved when the mother country was at war. In Toronto, as in most other parts of the country, many welcomed the news. In a spirit of celebration, people cheered as joyous bands thumping out "Rule Britannia" marched smartly down Yonge Street. Young men eager to serve king and country stormed hastily set up recruiting centres. Stirred by both the call to duty and the lure of adventure, Bethune was among the first to enlist.

He chose the Royal Canadian Army Medical Corps and after a brief training period, found himself with thousands of other volunteers heading across the Atlantic aboard the S.S. *Cassandra*. In England there was still more training, and drill, drill and more drill. Bethune soon became restless, craving excitement. When his unit received some new ambulances, he quickly offered to test drive one, and on his first outing, completely destroyed the vehicle in an accident. To the amazement of witnesses, he calmly emerged from the wreckage and walked away unhurt. This scrape with death seems to have temporarily satisfied his craving for dramatic action.

*Bethune in the Royal Navy, 1918*

Before long he had another chance. In February, 1915, his unit reached France where, as a stretcher-bearer, he was assigned to a mobile field unit that responded to emergency calls to carry the wounded back from the trenches.

Less than two months after his arrival at the front, the Second Battle of Ypres began. The German High Command was eager to try a deadly secret weapon—poisonous chlorine gas—on the enemy. For this experiment they chose the town of Ypres as the testing ground. April 22 was a clear, windless day in and around Ypres. Toward the late afternoon, German artillery shells began to rain on the British, French and Canadian troops holding the trench lines around Ypres. Then at 5:30 p.m., a greenish-yellow cloud started to creep eerily along the ground toward the Allied trenches. When it reached the French section of the line, men writhed, and pitched forward, clutching their throats and gagging. The gas had entered their lungs slashing like a knife, causing them to throw up violently. Panic-stricken and in terrible pain, many choked to death on their vomit. The fortunate ones stumbled out of the trenches and ran pell-mell to the rear, away from the engulfing death.

Within minutes the gas attack had punched a giant gap in the Allied line, and for a moment, it seemed that a German breakthrough was unavoidable. Fortunately for the Allies, the Germans were not aware of how successful their new weapon had been. Slow to move forward, they were thrown back by courageous, determined troops of the 1st Canadian Division, who had rushed forward to fill the hole. At a shocking cost in lives lost, the Canadians grimly held on until French and British forces relieved them forty-eight hours later.

Bethune's unit was called to the battle. With one out of every three Canadians killed or wounded, he and his comrades in the Medical Corps were in constant demand, and were themselves under heavy fire. On the morning of April 29, as Bethune was advancing toward the trenches, a piece of German shrapnel ripped into his left leg. The stretcher fell from his hands as he staggered, collapsing in the soft grey mud of the battlefield. When he regained consciousness, he found himself in a field hospital bed well behind the firing lines. Two days later, he was taken to a hospital ship. After three months in an English hospital, he reported again for duty, but to his disappointment, he was not sent back to France. Instead, he was told to return to Canada to complete his medical studies. Doctors were harder to find than stretcher-bearers.

He arrived in Toronto in November to enter a crash course to complete his degree. Just before Christmas, 1916, Norman Bethune graduated at a special convocation of the University of Toronto. His classmate during that final year was Frederick Banting, soon to become famous as one of the discoverers of insulin.

*Graduation, University of Toronto, 1916*

Bethune did not immediately return to Europe after graduation. Instead, he eagerly accepted an offer to substitute for two Stratford, Ontario, doctors who wanted to go on a long holiday. It was his first opportunity to practise medicine.

By April he was back home in Toronto. One day as he was walking down the street, a woman stepped in front of him, blocking his path. Why, she angrily demanded, was such a young, healthy man in Toronto? Why wasn't he overseas serving his country? Before he could reply, she grasped the lapel of his jacket and pinned to it a white feather, the symbol of cowardice.

The incident must have stung him. Certainly he was not a coward, but the woman could hardly have known that. Yet it was true, he realized, that while he was enjoying the mild Ontario spring, Canadians were losing their lives in France and Belgium. By the time he reached home, he had made a decision to return to the war, but not the army. Eager for change, he enlisted in the Royal Navy.

In September, 1917, Surgeon-Lieutenant Norman Bethune was aboard H.M.S. *Pegasus*, an aircraft carrier on patrol duty in the North Sea. Here he remained until the end of the war in November, 1918.

In January, 1919, back in civilian clothes after leaving naval headquarters in London, England, he considered his future. The smell of death in the trenches and the thrill of action at sea were too recent to forget. He was not emotionally ready to settle down, and the thought of returning to Canada to practise medicine in some quiet, small Ontario town turned him off. And besides, he had fallen in love with London. Its art galleries, theatres and nightclubs, the masses of people on its crowded streets beckoned to him. And London had another practical attraction—its medical training centres were among the world's finest.

Partly because he loved children, Bethune decided to study pediatrics and in February, 1919, he began his internship at the famous Hospital for Sick Children on Great Ormond Street.

*Group photo, Great Ormond Street Hospital for Sick Children, London*

But by autumn his mood had changed sharply. In contrast to his attitude in the spring, he was now fed up with London and homesick. He longed to see friends and family. Returning to Canada, he again substituted for several months for the Stratford doctors, and then for another in the town of Ingersoll.

Too soon the doctor he had been replacing returned and Bethune was without a job. At this point he came across an advertisement for the recently formed Canadian Air Force, and the thought of new adventure seized him. In Camp Borden, Ontario, he was made a flight-lieutenant in the medical service, a position he held for six months until boredom turned his attention back to London, England. He asked for a leave of absence.

He began his second London internship at Christmas, 1920. This time he would stay much longer. For the next three years he worked in several British hospitals gaining knowledge in various areas of medicine. He became fascinated with surgery, and passed the examinations that gained him his Fellowship in the Royal College of Surgeons in Edinburgh, Scotland.

On this return to London he met Frances Campbell Penney, the beautiful daughter of a well-known Edinburgh family. Frances, who was three years younger than Bethune, had had a private school education, and had attended fashionable finishing schools in Dresden and Paris. She wrote and spoke French, knew English literature, and was musical and artistic. Until she met Bethune she had never been serious about any man. The two fell in love.

*With his wife, Frances Campbell Penney*

In the summer of 1923, after Bethune had finished his final course, they were married in London. Then they went on a carefree, expensive, six-month honeymoon that took them to Italy, Austria and France. By the late winter of 1924, they had spent almost all of the large amount of money that Frances had inherited just before the marriage. At this point, they snapped out of their dream. They needed money, and quickly. The answer was to leave for North America so Bethune could start a medical practice. This, they hoped, would provide them with an income to allow them to live the good life.

# Chapter 2
# Michigan and New York

*With friends in Montreal, 1928*

Detroit, 1924: bustling, vigorous, expanding: booming with prosperity built on the automobile. The dream of rapid success lured Bethune to Detroit. With high hopes and the little remaining money from Frances's inheritance, he opened a consulting office close to the downtown area. Then he waited . . . and waited. Gradually patients began to trickle in, but many were poorly paid labourers or unemployed immigrants unable to pay for medical services.

When he realized that his practice was not going to grow as quickly as he had hoped, Bethune applied for a teaching position at the Detroit College of Medicine and Surgery. The best that he could get was a part-time appointment as a lecturer in prescription writing. Hardly fitting for a promising young physician and surgeon trained in the best London hospitals, but with his mounting debts, he had little choice. And he did well. At the end of the course, the medical students voted him their best teacher.

Shortly after accepting the teaching job, his luck began to change. In the spring of 1925 he received an appointment at Harper Hospital where, for the first time, he could practise surgery. As he became better known in the medical community, other physicians sent Bethune their patients who needed operations. Soon his office was filled, now with patients who could afford to pay. In a short time, his debts were gone. With his bank balance keeping pace with his rapidly growing practice, Bethune cheerfully spent the money. He bought a car, rented a fashionable apartment, and began to buy paintings, one of his favourite and most expensive hobbies.

He was living well but he had to work hard to earn his fees. Often called out in the middle of the night, he would return to catch no more than an hour or two of sleep. As a result, he had little time to spend with Frances. She had no friends and was lonely in Detroit. She also disliked the city. Soon they began to quarrel, and she left him to stay with friends in Canada. After several months, in response to Bethune's long, pleading letters, she reluctantly came back to Detroit.

Her return brought about no change in his habits. He seemed to be working even harder than before she had left. Then he started to complain to Frances of being tired and short of breath. Finally, in the autumn of 1926, he had a thorough physical examination. Stunned and angry, he came home to Frances clutching the medical report. He had pulmonary (lung) tuberculosis. The report staggered both of them. Was this a grim penalty for two years' hard work? They both knew that he had no choice. The disease was so serious that he would have to stop working and become a patient in a sanatorium.

Soon he was on a train en route to Trudeau Sanatorium, just outside the town of Saranac Lake in New York State. Bethune stared blankly through the window at the snow-covered slopes of the Adirondack Mountains. One idea kept racing through his mind: he didn't deserve this cruel blow of fate, nor was he ready to accept six months of rest in a hospital bed.

His doctors had other ideas. When he arrived at Trudeau, he received another medical examination. Then he was promptly put to bed in the infirmary and ordered to stay there. It was Christmas, 1926.

Bethune, who hated rules, unless they were his own, made it clear that he did not want to stay in bed. Acting on the doctors' orders, the nurses were forced to treat him as a prisoner. Bethune's answer was to wait until their backs were turned. Then he would pull his bathrobe over his shoulders, slip out of bed and reach for his cane. Setting his high hat on his head at a rakish angle, he sauntered casually down the halls paying visits to his highly amused fellow patients in other rooms.

In January his doctors agreed to release him from the infirmary, and he moved into one of the several cottages nestled among the tall fir trees on the sloping hospital grounds. Patients slept in the cottages, but took their meals in the main building. Among his five cottage mates was Dr. John Barnwell, a young American who became his closest friend.

Tuberculosis (TB) is one of history's oldest and most deadly killers. Sometimes known as the "white plague," for

centuries it had resisted the many attempts of medical science to discover its cure. In the 1920s people feared tuberculosis as cancer is feared today. The most common method of treating the disease was by taking patients away from polluted cities to sanatoriums in tranquil, rural settings. There, by breathing the fresh air and by doing nothing but resting, some patients were cured. One of the best-known sanatoriums in North America was at Saranac Lake. Its founder, Dr. Edward Livingston Trudeau, believed that bed rest was absolutely necessary to cure tuberculosis. The less the lung was exercised, the smaller the chance that the infection would spread.

Bethune was not always prepared to let medical theory interfere with his pleasure. Restless and eager to escape at least for a few hours from the confinement of the sanatorium, he persuaded four of his fellow patients to join him in a caper. Discovering that Dr. Barnwell, whose bed was closest to the window, had a ski jacket, Bethune stuffed it with blankets and placed it under the bed covers to resemble a sleeping person. When the nurse, who patrolled the cottages at night, shone her flashlight in the window, she saw what she thought was the doctor asleep in his bed. At that very moment, Bethune, Barnwell and four companions, who had silently scaled the fence, were well down the road merrily on their way to Saranac Lake for a night on the town.

These good times ended abruptly when he received a letter from Frances telling him that she was leaving him to go back to Scotland. Though her decision was not entirely unexpected, it hurt Bethune deeply. At the same time, he had to face another pressing problem: he needed money badly. Despite her decision to leave him, Bethune felt obligated to support Frances financially. He also had to meet his hospital and other bills. There seemed to be no choice. In March he left Trudeau Sanatorium and returned to Detroit.

Unable to find a doctor to manage his practice when he went to Saranac Lake, he had had to abandon it. Now, with teaching the only possible source of income, he took up his former position. But the strain was too great. During a series of lectures he was giving to his classes, his tuberculosis grew worse and he broke down. By the early summer he was back at Trudeau hoping to recover his strength. There he suffered still another setback. Only days after returning, he received a letter from a Detroit lawyer. Frances had sued for divorce.

For several months Bethune grew more and more depressed. Gone were the carefree nights of partying in town. His outlook turned black as he came to believe that there was no escape from an early death. He started to speak openly of suicide. But he did not give up hope entirely. Day after day, he spent long hours in the Trudeau library poring over books on tuberculosis. One day he came across an article in a medical journal that described a method of treatment called artificial pneumothorax. The process was simple. A hollow needle was inserted between the ribs into the chest cavity. When air was pumped through the needle, the air pressure caused the lung to collapse. Once at rest, the diseased lung would heal and function normally again.

Hastily picking up the book, he rushed out of the library to search for his doctor. When he found him, he explained his discovery and then demanded that they go directly to the operating room.

*Bethune always stood out in a crowd*

To his surprise, he found that the doctor knew about artificial pneumothorax and considered the method much too dangerous. The needle might puncture the lung and so cause greater damage. He turned Bethune down.

But Bethune was not put off that easily. He strode to the office of Dr. Lawrason Brown, the director of Trudeau Sanatorium, and made his case again. Finally, worn down by Bethune's persistent demands, Dr. Brown agreed to call a meeting of the medical staff to hear Bethune's argument. At the meeting, after Bethune had fully explained why he should receive artificial pneumothorax, the director once again impatiently underlined the risks. At this point Bethune, in his most theatrical way, unbuttoned his shirt to bare his chest and announced: "Gentlemen, I welcome the risk." After a short conference with his colleagues, Dr. Brown told a triumphant Bethune that his wish would be granted.

He danced back to the cottage and boasted of his achievement to his mates. When he had finished, Dr. Barnwell cautiously handed him a letter. Bethune carelessly tore open the envelope and unfolded the single page. Suddenly his smile turned to a frown as he read the brief note. The letter was from Frances. The divorce had been granted. Though the news was not a surprise, it still shocked him. He abruptly left the cottage and walked out into the cold night air to be alone.

Three days later the artificial pneumothorax operation was performed. It was October 24, 1927. With one lung almost totally collapsed, he walked slowly out of the operating room and began to climb the steep hill that led to the cottage. Refusing the offer of help, though gasping for breath, he staggered the distance of more than a hundred metres to his room. He would not admit that he was suffering great pain.

Late that afternoon his doctor arrived to check on Bethune's condition, expecting to find him in bed. Opening the door, he looked up to see Bethune standing on a chair that had been set on a table. He was painting on a sheet of laundry paper nearly two metres wide that stretched for almost twenty metres around the cottage walls. When completed, the mural, which he called "A T.B.'s Progress," told the story of Bethune's life . . . and death. It pictures him as a boy pursued by a tubercle bacillus (germ) that finally catches and infects him. He tries every means of escape, but fails. The last of the nine panels shows a graveyard with his tombstone and one for each of his cottage mates. He asked them to predict the dates of their deaths. He chose his own as 1932.

Then, what must have seemed like a miracle occurred. Before he finished the mural several days later, his shortness of breath had vanished. Within weeks his condition improved remarkably; his right lung had healed while the left lung remained stable. In early December he was released from Trudeau Sanatorium.

The experience of tuberculosis and his enforced stay in the sanatorium had a profound effect on Bethune's outlook on life. Despite his efforts to resist bed rest, he had been forced to remain inactive. This had given him an opportunity to think. Lying in his cottage bed or during strolls in the woods, he was able to examine his past and to look into his own heart and mind in an effort to plan his future. Referring to a tubercular patient, he later wrote:

*In the sanatorium, perhaps for the first time, he has the opportunity to think. Contemplation becomes a substitution for action. The result is a deepening of his intellectual and spiritual life.*

His battle with tuberculosis had changed his view of success. Until his sickness, he had been selfish and had concentrated all his efforts on earning money.

*Dr. Edward Archibald*

Before leaving, he told one of his fellow patients, "I'm going to find something I can do for the human race, something great, and I am going to do it before I die."

Bethune's plan of action was made in those days of recovery from the artificial pneumothorax treatment. He had had tuberculosis, he had studied all the available literature at Trudeau, and he had spent hours discussing the disease with the doctors. Now his path was clear. He would dedicate his life to the study of this dreaded killer disease.

He did not have to travel far. The leading Canadian authority on tuberculosis, and a pioneer in chest surgery, was Dr. Edward Archibald of Montreal's Royal Victoria Hospital. He often visited Trudeau Sanatorium. Impressed by Bethune and his qualifications, he agreed to accept him as an assistant in training after his release.

# Chapter 3
# Montreal

Bethune arrived in Montreal with high hopes. Truly confident that he could indeed do "something great for the human race," he aimed high. His goal was to make a breakthrough in the search for a cure for tuberculosis. He had reason to believe that he was suited for the task. By nature he was unusually inquisitive. He delighted in analyzing puzzling questions and coming up with solutions. Eager to discover how things worked, he loved taking them apart. He also had considerable skill with his hands. All these were essential requirements in both the laboratory and the operating room.

Dr. Archibald saw these qualities in his assistant, and gave him almost a free hand in the laboratories of the Royal Victoria Hospital. During his five years there, Bethune spent much of his time working with chemists, laboratory technicians, and specialists in various fields of medicine. His research was varied, but his greatest contribution was the large number of surgical instruments that he designed and tested for use in thoracic (chest) surgery. Among the many were the Bethune rib shears, which are still used today. Another was the Bethune artificial pneumothorax apparatus. The Pilling Company of Philadelphia, which manufactured and sold Bethune's instruments to surgeons around the world, needed a full page in its 1932 catalogue to list and describe his inventions.

*Royal Victoria Hospital*

He began to study thoracic surgery by watching, and later assisting, Dr. Archibald. These were the pioneering days in chest surgery and the operating room was no place for the squeamish. The scene was always bloody.

The artificial pneumothorax treatment could not always be used to cure tubercular patients. Sometimes, the patient had to be operated on. First, the surgeon made the opening incision, a long slash from under the shoulder around to the chest. Next he removed the ribs, often as many as three in a single operation. Then he sewed the patient up. The purpose of this operation, known as a thoracoplasty, was to remove support from the chest wall. This allowed the diseased part of the lung to collapse and go into a state of rest. If all went well, in time it would heal.

The quality of anesthetic in the 1930s was much poorer than that used today. Because surgeons did not like to keep their patients under too long, they had to work quickly. Bethune soon gained a reputation as an exceptionally rapid operator. He would often amaze his assistants and the students he taught at McGill University by looking at the clock, announcing the length of time for the operation, and finishing within seconds of his deadline.

Many of the older doctors viewed his performances as showmanship that had no place in the operating room. Too much speed, they argued, could result in serious errors, even in the loss of the patient. They also criticized him for other reasons. Driven by his curiosity, Bethune was forever questioning everything, including medical and surgical techniques that doctors had been using for years. To him, tradition was a mask that often concealed error. Never satisfied with the answer, "That's how it's done," he demanded reasons. Some doctors, who were deeply offended by his criticism, believed that he was attacking them personally, not their ideas.

In addition, his habit of saying exactly what he felt was annoying. He once shocked a meeting of Montreal doctors by openly questioning his own chief, Dr. Archibald. Everyone else considered Archibald beyond criticism.

Gradually, most doctors and nurses shied away from Bethune. They considered him too self-willed, stubbornly opinionated, and dangerously outspoken. Finally, even Dr. Archibald could no longer tolerate him. He was critical of

Bethune's operational techniques, which he blamed for the loss of several patients' lives. In personality, character and temperament, Bethune and Archibald were direct opposites. One evening at a party, Bethune said to Archibald, "Oh, what's the use. I'll never manage to explain anything to you. The trouble is that, by nature, you shoot butterflies with a shotgun and I like to hunt elephants with a bow and arrow." After five years of working together, Dr. Archibald asked Bethune to leave the Royal Victoria Hospital.

*Bethune assisting Archibald*

Behind Dr. Archibald's disappointment with Bethune the surgeon, was his failure to understand Bethune, the man. He was not alone. Even those who admired him were often mystified by his strange, often contradictory personal behaviour. He seemed to thrive on opposites. His taste in clothing was an example. When most doctors were conservatively dressed in grey suits, white shirts and plain ties, Bethune frequently wore slacks, sport jackets and coloured shirts or turtleneck sweaters.

Another example was his choice of friends. He often spoke proudly of the royal officials and bishops in his aristocratic family tree, which he claimed to be able to trace back for nearly a millennium. But he found himself more at home with poor artists, students and writers.

Bethune loved to criticize mainstream society. He complained that many people, especially the rich, were boring. They led dull, mechanical and unproductive lives. They did nothing but follow the rules dictated by society. In contrast, he preferred to reveal his feelings openly and to act freely. He was entirely aware of, and deeply amused by the fact that his unconventional behaviour usually shocked people.

Once when he was taking a shower in his apartment, he heard the doorbell ring. When the bell continued to ring insistently, Bethune stepped out of the shower, walked to the door, and opened it. The sight of the unclothed, dripping wet Bethune so unnerved the callers that they fled. At times he behaved almost childishly in offending people he disliked.

Once when he was with a friend, he excused himself, saying, "I just saw _____ come in. I can't stand him. I'll be back as soon as I can irritate him."

Though a few people secretly admired him for his courage in speaking his mind and criticizing people to their faces, his openness did not make him popular. His bold manner and unpredictable behaviour reduced his circle of friends. He was isolating himself from the society he criticized.

Bethune's reaction to his dismissal by Dr. Archibald was double-edged. Just when his international reputation was growing, he had been forced out of one of North America's finest hospitals. Yet he also saw the dismissal as an opportunity. Although he knew that he owed much to Dr. Archibald for his knowledge of chest surgery, Bethune had never been satisfied to be just an assistant. He was not a follower. He longed to set up his own clinic, where he would have to answer to no one.

He was in luck. Sacred Heart Hospital in Cartierville, just north of Montreal, was looking for a surgeon. In the late winter of 1933 he was appointed Chief of the Department of Thoracic Surgery. At last he was on his own. When he left three years later, having trained two young doctors as fully qualified thoracic surgeons to carry on his work, he felt justifiably proud of his achievement.

His personal life was less rewarding. After his divorce in 1927, he grew lonely for Frances and begged her to come back to him. Two years later, she finally gave in and they were married again. But the second marriage was no more successful than the first. It ended in divorce just after Bethune began work at Sacred Heart.

He tried to compensate for this loss, the most serious of his life, by finding other outlets for his energy and talent. He started to write poetry and short stories. Unsatisfied, he turned to painting, and was good enough to have his work shown at exhibitions in Montreal.

It was his interest in art that helped reduce the pain of his childless marriage. Scraping together some money for supplies, he persuaded the gifted Montreal artist, Fritz Brandtner, to teach children who were unable to afford private art lessons. Using his apartment as a studio, Bethune formed the Montreal Children's' Creative Art Centre. Here on Saturday mornings, working-class children came to learn how to paint in watercolours and oils.

The joy that the success of the art school brought to Bethune was temporary. He was uneasy about his future and unsatisfied by his past. There had, of course, been achievements, but all too often they were followed by setbacks. Restless, as usual, he was looking for meaning in life. In his search, he began to become aware of the effects of the Depression.

A worldwide economic slump had begun soon after the dramatic collapse of the New York stock market in October, 1929. Within months, even those who had not invested money in stocks or bonds

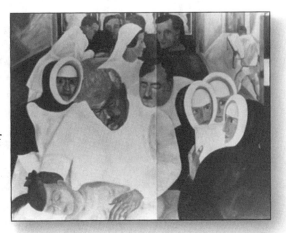

*Fritz Brandtner's painting of Bethune at Sacred Heart Hospital*

were caught in the fallout from the market crash. People became afraid of using their savings; they cut back on their spending and began to buy only food and other necessities. The result was a sharp drop in the demand for goods. When already overstocked factories reduced or stopped production, thousands of workers found themselves without work.

Unlike today, there were no government welfare agencies to provide unemployment insurance and family allowances, or to pay for hospital and doctor bills. In city streets, long lines of shabbily dressed, unemployed men waiting for a free bowl of soup became as common a sight as "No Help Wanted" signs on factory fences. Idle men with empty stomachs, their heads bowed in despair, sat dejectedly on park benches or on street curbs, symbolizing the grim way of life for hundreds of thousands of Canadians.

At first, Bethune was too involved in his own personal world to notice the suffering around him. He became aware, however, through his growing interest in literature and art that brought him into contact with writers, artists and poets. These creative people he met shared one common emotion—a bitter anger against a society and a government that seemed unable or unwilling to combat the paralyzing poverty and unemployment that gripped Canada. Night after night, Bethune was the host at his apartment for gatherings that usually ended in the early morning hours. The talk would often turn to unemployment, soup kitchens, and

*Self-portrait, 1935*

*Students at the Montreal Children's Creative Art Centre*

the growing misery and discontent in society. When it did, it would usually end with fierce criticism of capitalism, the political and economic system that most of Bethune's friends believed was the cause of the Depression.

These concerns were entirely new to him. Never before had he paid serious attention to politics or economics. Now they gradually took on meaning because they opened his eyes to a side of health care that he had ignored. Inspired by ideas that came from the endless evening discussions, he started to realize that sickness and its cure were often linked to a patient's income. It was certainly true of tubercular patients; most of them came from poor homes. They lived in crowded, badly heated and unsanitary rooms. Without money, they could afford neither medicine nor visits to a doctor. Only when the disease had advanced too far, did they go, in desperation, for medical help. By contrast, when well-to-do people developed symptoms of disease, they rarely delayed going to a doctor. For this reason, they were often cured. Bethune kept turning over in his mind an old saying of Dr. Trudeau's that now held deep meaning for him: "There is a rich man's tuberculosis and a poor man's tuberculosis. The difference between the two is that the rich man recovers and the poor man dies."

Bethune was developing a social conscience. Until now he had believed that scientific and medical discoveries would eventually rid the world of disease. The real evil, he soon came to believe, was the political and economic organization of society.

Once he had adopted these new ideas, he acted, as always, with passion and a firm belief in what he had to do: like a missionary, he would spread the word. The first to hear his message were his medical colleagues. In speeches and articles he hammered out the same themes. Better living conditions had to be created for the poor. More sanatoriums had to be built so half-cured patients would not be sent home too soon in order to make way for others in need of treatment. Schoolchildren must have compulsory tuberculosis tests, and nurses, nursemaids, and food handlers must be given regular physical examinations to ensure that they were not infected. Soon he was invited to speak to Montreal service clubs and social groups. His audiences would nod approval and applaud, but in most cases they would soon forget.

It was not long before he realized that his ideas were impractical without government support. The reforms he was calling for required large sums of money. In the midst of the Depression, people had little money to spare, and private businessmen were unwilling to invest in his ideas. This left government as the only source of the money that was needed, and in the 1930s very few people believed that government should undertake projects such as those proposed by Bethune.

Canadians were deeply suspicious of political and economic systems in which governments had a large amount of power. They watched in fear two such systems in Europe: communism and fascism. Despite huge differences between them, the systems were strikingly similar in one respect: they were opposed to democracy. Communism in the Soviet Union (Russia), and fascism in Italy and Germany had ended free elections and stripped their citizens of many rights that Canadians believed were the basis of a free society. As a result, most people in Canada supported the idea that the best government was the one that governed least. It was against this background that Bethune was trying to make a case for socialized medicine. The odds were against him.

Aware that he was getting nowhere, he became frustrated and angry. Then in the summer of 1935 he accepted an offer to accompany several colleagues to the Soviet Union to attend a scientific congress in Moscow and Leningrad. On the trip, Bethune spent much of his time visiting Russian hospitals to learn their methods for treating tuberculosis.

He was even more interested in their system of medical and hospital care. Known today as medicare, it was then called socialized medicine. In the 1930s, all Russian clinics and hospitals were managed by government. Anyone, regardless of income, could receive medical attention at no cost. Bethune was deeply impressed, yet he also recognized that the Soviet Union was not a paradise. In many technical areas, he and other Canadian doctors were ahead of the Russians. He was also disturbed by the strict regulations that controlled Soviet society. Still, he was inspired by the Soviet promise of equal medical care for all.

He returned to Montreal in September eager to preach these new ideas to the medical profession and the public. In a series of speeches he argued that health was a public, not a private matter. It was the duty of government to preserve and maintain the health of its citizens. To achieve this, doctors should not work on a fee-for-service basis. Their consultation offices and operating rooms should be open to all patients. Payment to doctors should be made by government. He told one group of doctors:

> *Socialized medicine and the abolition or restriction of private practice would appear to be the realistic solution of the problem. Let us take the profit, the private economic profit, out of Medicine, and purify our profession of rapacious individualism. Let us make it disgraceful to enrich ourselves at the expense of the miseries of our fellow men.*

Around him he gathered doctors, nurses, social workers and laypersons who shared his ideas. Calling themselves the Montreal Group for the Security of the People's Health, they met regularly at Bethune's apartment, to study the medical systems of most European countries, the United States and Canada. Their purpose was to work out a system that would ensure that all Canadians received proper health care. By the summer of 1936 they had developed four basic experimental plans. All had one aspect in common—they were to be run by the government, which would pay the doctors and medical workers.

The approaching Quebec provincial election seemed to Bethune the ideal opportunity to publicly launch this pioneering effort in the campaign for socialized medicine in Canada. On the eve of the election, Bethune's group printed and circulated their plans among medical workers and opposition politicians, and to the government. Bethune, ever optimistic, was unprepared for the reaction. Most doctors were hostile, fearing that under Bethune's plans they would become government employees. Many religious authorities and most politicians believed that socialized medicine belonged to communism, and had no place in Canada.

Bethune was shocked and disappointed. He and others had worked for months to develop ideas they believed would save lives and lessen suffering, yet they were turned down simply because people who had a different political system were using them.

The hostile public reaction had another effect on Bethune. It seemed to justify a decision he had made a few months earlier. For some time he had listened to the views of liberals, socialists and communists without being able to accept any particular political philosophy. Then came the trip to the Soviet Union. He found he had much in common with the Russian communists. Like him they rejected out-of-date traditions. They too believed in making bold and dramatic changes to achieve their aims, and were ready to act on their beliefs, unlike others who criticized but did nothing. Despite being deeply troubled by the absence of individual freedoms in Soviet society, Bethune quietly joined the Communist party of Canada in November 1935. Knowing that public knowledge of his political commitment could endanger his position in the Roman Catholic Sacred Heart Hospital, he had kept his decision a secret that he shared with only a few party officials.

Now in the summer of 1936, with his proposals for socialized medicine rejected by politicians, the public and, most disappointingly, his own profession, Bethune felt alone and alienated.

*Bethune in 1935*

*The caption reads: "To Mitzi and Fritz [Brandtner] with love & kisses. Norman Bethune Jan. 18/36"*

# Chapter 4
# Spain

Just weeks later, Bethune gazed at the vanishing skyline of Quebec City from the rail of the S.S. *Empress of Britain*. He was on his way to Spain carrying a load of medical supplies and a letter of introduction to the Spanish prime minister. Before he left, a friend had asked him why, at age forty-six, he had given up his hospital position to try to help people he did not know and whose language he did not speak. His answer was brief: "I'm going to Spain because it is in Spain that the real issues of our time are going to be fought out. It is there that democracy will either die or survive."

The Spanish Civil War had begun on July 18 with an armed rebellion led by General Francisco Franco, head of the Spanish army, who called on the people of Spain to support him. His aim was to overthrow the left-leaning government that had come to power in a free, democratic election in February. Many Spaniards supported Franco, but many others passionately opposed him and pledged their loyalty to the elected government.

*Bethune en route to Spain*

Within a week, Franco's revolution had become a civil war. On his side were most of the army personnel, the leaders of the Catholic Church, big businessmen, wealthy landowners, and the Falange, the Spanish fascist party. These became known as the Nationalists. In the opposite camp were a few loyal army leaders and units, the navy and the air force, most factory and farm workers, and the leading intellectuals. The majority of Spanish liberals, as well as groups further to the left (socialists, anarchists, and communists) stood firmly on the side of the government. These were called the Loyalists.

Franco soon received pre-arranged military aid from Nazi Germany and Fascist Italy. Both Hitler and Mussolini wanted a chance to test their new dive bombers and tanks on Spanish civilians. By August, airplanes of the German Condor Legion were in the skies over Spain, while on the ground, Italian tanks and troops were fighting beside Nationalist soldiers. To counter this, the Spanish government called on the Soviet Union to send assistance. In contrast to the massive contributions made by the Germans and Italians, Russian aid, in the form of technical advisers and a few tanks and planes, was pitifully small.

The Spanish Civil War became big news everywhere. Foreign observers flocked to Spain to report developments. Newspaper reporters, writers, photographers and filmmakers sent their impressions of events back to their own countries. Both sides in the conflict had followers outside Spain. A great many Catholics, and millions of people afraid of communism cheered on Franco's Nationalists. Many others, including Bethune, sympathized with the Loyalists. To him their cause represented the struggle of a freely elected democratic government against the rising world movement of fascism.

As the news from Spain became blacker, Bethune was weighing his present and future plans against events in Spain. Finally, he decided to offer himself for service there. When he approached the International Red Cross and learned they had refused to intervene in a civil war, he began to look elsewhere. In his search, he came across an organization called The Committee to Aid Spanish Democracy. It had just been formed to send medical workers and supplies to the Loyalists. He volunteered and was immediately accepted.

When Bethune reached Madrid on November 3, the city was under siege. On two sides of the capital, Franco's troops were massing for an imminent attack, while from above, German dive bombers terrorized the city. In his room in the Gran Via Hotel, Bethune met Henning Sorensen, a multilingual Canadian who agreed to act as his interpreter. During the next few days, as Nationalist troops began their major assault, Bethune and Sorensen made a tour of the major hospitals. He was warmly greeted everywhere and assured of work as a surgeon.

But this was not what he wanted. He had not given up a hospital position in Montreal to exchange it for one in Madrid. As always, he was searching for a role where he would not only

*Henning Sorensen*

*Bethune's mobile unit delivered blood everywhere along the thousand-kilometre front*

be useful, but also attract attention. Conscious of the need for publicity in order to raise money in Canada, he knew the importance of press coverage. A plan began to form in his mind, and one day he turned to Sorensen and said, "Henning, I've got an idea. We'll start a blood transfusion service." Then he unfolded the scheme that he had been working on for several days.

It had two important advantages. Because the blood transfusion service would be the first of its kind, it would attract the foreign news correspondents. In addition, other groups, such as the Scots and the English, had formed their own ambulance units. Why shouldn't the Canadians in Spain do the same and also provide a project for Canadians at home to support? The Spanish government promised their enthusiastic support for his proposal, and Bethune sent a telegram to the Canadian Committee to Aid Spanish Democracy informing them of his decision. Without waiting for an answer, he confidently set off for England with Sorensen to buy supplies.

In London they bought a station wagon, a small refrigerator, a sterilizing unit, blood flasks, serums, surgical instruments and other supplies. They also added a member to their new blood transfusion unit. The driver of the station wagon on the trip back through the English countryside to the coast, was Hazen Sise, a young Canadian architect whom they had met in

London. Sise was so impressed by Bethune and his plans that he closed his office and joined him.

When they returned to Madrid, the Spanish government supplied them with a large, second-floor apartment in an upper-middle class neighbourhood. The location was relatively safe from bombs, since the German planes usually attacked the working-class sectors of Madrid. Bethune named the unit *Servicio canadiense de Transfusión de Sangre* (Canadian Blood Transfusion Service). In addition to the three Canadians, there were: an American laboratory technician, Celia Greenspan, four Spanish doctors, four nurses, four office workers, and a cook. Before the new transfusion service could start operating, they had to attract blood donors. To get these they made appeals on radio and in Madrid newspapers.

*Hazen Sise*

The *Servicio canadiense* opened its doors just before Christmas, 1936. On that first morning, the Canadians went to the window, hearing a commotion in the street below. As they looked out, lined up as far as they could see were people who had come to donate blood. Their appeals had been heard.

The crowd was so large that the unit was unable to process everyone the first day. Each volunteer was given a medical examination, and a sample of blood was taken. If the sample showed

*With Sise and Sorensen, Madrid, 1936*

that the volunteer had no diseases, he or she was called back to give five hundred cubic centimetres of blood. In exchange, each donor received a cup of coffee and a letter allowing the person to buy extra food. Once blood was taken, the donor's name, the blood type and the date were typed on a label attached to the bottle. A sodium citrate solution was added to the blood to prevent clotting, and the bottle was then placed in a refrigerator.

For the first two months, the *Servicio canadiense* delivered blood by request to many of the more than fifty Madrid hospitals. Bethune knew the need for blood was just as great outside the city, and when Franco, unable to crush Madrid, shifted his troops and eased the pressure on the capital, Bethune was given permission to extend his operations.

*The English station wagon after a coat of camouflaging paint*

Early in February he, Sise, and an Englishman named Thomas Worsley, drove east to Barcelona to complete plans for supplying front-line hospitals. When they learned that a major Loyalist defeat had taken place at Málaga on the southern coast, and that many refugees were fleeing from the disaster, Bethune decided to drive to the battle.

Filling the truck with bottles of blood, they drove south to Almería, one hundred and fifty kilometres northeast of Málaga. As they were delivering their cargo of blood, they were warned to go no farther. Málaga had fallen, and Italian and Nationalist troops were marching toward Almería.

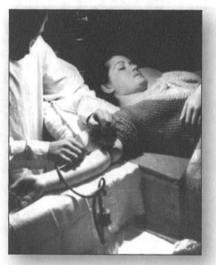

*Taking blood from a Spanish donor in Madrid*

Ignoring this advice, Bethune turned the truck west on the road to Málaga. Within a short time they came upon small groups of people dragging themselves along the stone road. Then they met more and more, until they were passing an endless stream of men, women and children. Some were carrying blankets, food or a priceless household treasure that they had refused to leave behind. Others, exhausted, had left the procession of refugees and lay or sat helplessly by the roadside.

As they drove on, Bethune became angrier and angrier. Suddenly, he pulled the truck to a halt on the highway. He had made a decision: he and his companions would transport to safety as many of the refugees as they could. Getting out, he opened the rear doors of the truck and motioned to a limping child and her mother. Immediately men and women surrounded him, pushing, in an effort to find a space. Only when the shout of "*Niños y mujeres, solamente*" (Women and children only!) was repeated several times did the men draw back.

For three days and nights the three men drove, working in shifts as they raced back and forth to Almería with their pitiful human cargo.

When Bethune returned to Madrid, he wrote an article unleashing the intense hatred of the Fascists that had built up inside him during those seventy-two hours. Here he describes the last night:

*And now comes the final barbarism . . . When the little seaport of Almería was completely filled with refugees . . . we were heavily bombed by German and Italian Fascist airplanes . . . These planes made no effort to hit the government battleship in the harbour or bomb the barracks. They deliberately dropped ten great bombs in the very centre of the town where on the main street were sleeping, huddled together on the pavement so closely that a car could pass only with difficulty, the exhausted refugees. After the planes had passed I picked up in my arms three dead children from the pavement . . . where they had been standing in a great queue waiting for a cupful of preserved milk and a handful of dry bread, the only food some of them had for days. The street was a shambles of the dead and dying, lit only by the orange glare of burning buildings. In the darkness the moans of the wounded children, shrieks of agonized mothers, the curses of the men rose in a massed cry higher and higher to a pitch of intolerable intensity.*

*Standing by the Renault truck bought in France, 1937*

There could be no turning back. Haunted by the images of dead children, Bethune was determined to thrust his whole being into the war against fascism. By the end of the month, his transfusion unit was serving more than a hundred hospitals and casualty clearing stations. The unit, its name changed to *Instituto hispano-canadiense de Transfusión de Sangre* (Spanish-Canadian Blood Transfusion Institute), now had a staff of twenty-five. Bethune seemed to be everywhere on the thousand-kilometre front that the *Instituto* covered. A call would come from a front-line hospital at any time of night or day. He and his driver would hurriedly load the refrigerator with the required blood and race along the curving, dusty roads.

These trips were often dangerous, a fact that Bethune knew and actually

*Bethune and Sorensen take lunch with Spanish troops in the Sierra de Guadarrama, December 26, 1936*

*With refugee children from Málaga*

enjoyed. Called to the battle of Guadalajara in March, 1937, he took with him two filmmakers who were making a film on him and the *Instituto*. On the road they met retreating soldiers who warned them that Nationalist troops were in hot pursuit. Bethune thanked them and pushed on.

Soon, as warned, they came under fire. "Turn this truck around. Let's get out of here," one of the cameramen shouted.

Bethune shouted back, "I thought you came to film a war, not to run to the rear," and kept driving. At last, when bullets began flying past the truck, Bethune braked sharply and ordered his companions to jump. The order was hardly necessary; they threw themselves into the ditch beside the road, with Bethune following.

Later, after the firing had ended and they got back in the truck, they found a bullet hole in the windshield on the driver's side at the level of Bethune's throat.

Eventually the strain began to wear him down. His nerves were affected and sometimes he drank too much and became hard to work with. Complaints reached the Committee to Aid Spanish Democracy, and also the Communist Party.

And another old problem, Bethune's conflict with authority, reappeared. By early 1937, the Loyalist government was in the process of taking over the operation of all foreign units including the transfusion service. Bethune, the lone wolf, resisted, and arguments broke out between him and the Spanish authorities. It was time he left.

Even with his personal weaknesses, he was a hero to many Spaniards. The idea of taking bottled blood to front-line troops was not Bethune's. Others had dreamed of it before, but none had dared to try it. Bethune, dynamic and aggressive, and willing to take chances, was equal to the challenge. By risking his own life, he rushed blood to troops, instead of waiting for them to come to him. The mobile blood bank, his dramatic and timely solution to an ancient problem, was the greatest military-medical contribution made in the Spanish Civil War.

In May, he was asked to come home to go on a cross-country speaking tour. It was a convenient solution to his growing irritability. He had done his work in Spain and his assistants could carry on. Tired out and reluctant to return, yet anxious to leave Spain, he arrived in New York on June 6, 1937.

From the beginning, the tour was a success. Crowds in Toronto and Montreal greeted him triumphantly. Through the summer months he travelled across Canada, into the United States, and back again to Toronto.

At first he did not like the tour, and felt he was not speaking well. But as it progressed, the emotional meetings in crowded theatres, halls and arenas inspired him. Thousands of cheering people hung on his every word. His style of speaking improved, and he began to enjoy the crowds and their reaction to his message. Appearing at two and sometimes three meetings a day, he told of the work of the *Instituto*. He would explain how wounded soldiers, faint from the loss of blood, lay in their cots, seemingly lifeless, whiter almost than the sheets that covered them. As the transfused blood began to seep into their veins, colour would reappear in their cheeks, and they would begin to stir. A word would slowly form on their lips, and then a smile would gradually creep across their face.

He also described the horrors of war. Night after night he relived those days and nights on the road to Almería. His vivid memories, presented so clearly through his passionate words, deeply moved his audiences.

*Toronto newspaper clipping from Tuesday, June 15, 1937*

During the tour he announced that he would go back to Spain to expand the service of the *Instituto*. He had already decided against going back to Montreal. There he found nothing but closed doors. Just after his return from Spain, he had visited some of his old patients at Sacred Heart

*Members of the blood transfusion unit in Madrid, 1937*

Hospital. He was warmly greeted by his medical colleagues and patients, but not by the Catholic hospital officials. Their sympathies were clearly with Franco's Nationalists. Later, describing his visit to a friend, he tried to joke about it but the incident hurt him deeply. After his experience in Spain, he was unable to understand how anyone could be in favour of Franco.

They were not alone in rejecting Bethune because of his political beliefs. At the beginning of the tour, Bethune wanted to announce that he was a communist. The Committee to Aid Spanish Democracy, especially its communist members, forbade him to do so. As one of the sponsors of the tour, they argued that there were people who would not donate money if this fact were known. For a time Bethune knuckled under and agreed. He even denied his Communist Party membership when asked by reporters. At last, he refused to conceal it any longer. On July 20, 1937, at a banquet in Winnipeg, he boldly announced, "I have the honour to be a communist."

Now that it was known, many fellow doctors who had disliked him before, began to loathe him. At the same time he was also in trouble with the Communist Party. Like the medical profession, they were finding him a difficult rebel to discipline. He would accept no master.

*After his return from Spain, 1937*

The old restlessness had set in again. It was time to move on. But where? The answer came from an event that took place more than sixteen thousand kilometres away. On July 7, 1937, Japan attacked China. Just as Bethune had been attracted by events in Spain one year earlier, he was now becoming absorbed by what was happening in China.

# Chapter 5
# Shaanxi

Like most Canadians at the time, Bethune knew little about China. During the summer of 1937, as his interest grew, he soon became familiar with an outline of recent events. In 1931 Japanese troops had defeated Chinese forces and moved into the northern Chinese province of Manchuria. From there they began to make plans to move southward. General Chiang Kai-shek, leader of the Guomindang party that governed China, did little to resist the foreign invaders. Instead, his army concentrated on trying to eliminate Chiang's domestic enemy, the small but powerful Chinese Communist forces led by Mao Zedong.

Driven from southeastern China by Chiang's forces, Mao led his army, along with their wives and children, on a trek of 10,000 kilometres through treacherous swamps and arid deserts, across foaming rivers and over ice-covered mountains. Hounded by Chiang's troops, they had to fight battle after battle. Of the more than 100,000 who began, fewer than 20,000 reached Shaanxi province 386 days later. Early in 1936, these exhausted and scarred survivors arrived at the remote town of Yan'an, which would become the Communist base for the next ten years.

There these forces remained, even after a truce between Mao and Chiang Kai-shek was signed later the same year. Shortly after learning that the Chinese adversaries had signed a truce, the Japanese began the all-out attack on China that had caught Bethune's attention. In July, powerful Japanese forces rapidly drove the badly equipped and poorly trained Chinese armies south. A few months later, one of the most brutal massacres in modern warfare took place when the Japanese entered Nanjing, the defenceless capital city of China. Encouraged by their commanding officers, Japanese soldiers went on a wild rampage butchering men, women and children. The slaughter lasted several days.

While Bethune was on the speaking tour that summer, his mind had begun to focus on events in China. It quickly became clear to him that China was undergoing the same kind of struggle that was taking place in Spain. Unable to return to Spain, and unwilling to remain in Canada, he decided to offer his services to the Chinese.

In the autumn of 1937 he set off for New York to raise money for the trip. There, the recently formed China Aid Council promised him medical supplies and some financial support. Jean Ewen, a Canadian nurse who spoke Chinese, agreed to join him, and so did Dr. Charles Parsons, an American.

On January 8, 1938, Bethune, Jean Ewen and Parsons stood at the rail of the liner S.S. *Empress of Asia*, as it slowly pulled away from its mooring at the Vancouver docks. They were waving to a small group of friends who had come to see them off as they left for their three-week voyage to China.

From Hong Kong they flew to Wuhan, the temporary headquarters of Chiang Kai-shek's government. With air raid sirens sounding as they left their plane, they rushed to a shelter seconds before the arrival of Japanese bombers. After the all-clear, they were taken to meet Zhou Enlai, an important Communist official. When Bethune explained that he had come to China to join Mao's Communist Eighth Route Army, Zhou promised to make the arrangements. As they were about to leave three weeks later, Parsons, who would not work with the Communists, refused to go. Bethune and Ewen left without him.

On February 22 they set out for the Jin-Cha-Ji Border Region in Shanxi province, one of the two districts in northern China under Communist control. In peacetime they could have travelled the distance of thirteen hundred kilometres in a few days, but with Japanese troops streaming south and west, they were warned to prepare for a much longer trip.

Accompanied by a lone Eighth Route Army soldier as a guide, they took the crowded train north on the Beijing-Wuhan line to the rail junction city of Zhengzhou. There they spent the night in a shack near the railway station. Up early, they shoved their way onto another packed train heading west. The trip of fewer than three hundred kilometres to the city of Tongguan was slow and dangerous. Several times the train stopped without warning. The engineer had seen Japanese planes and was not taking any chances. Bethune, Ewen and

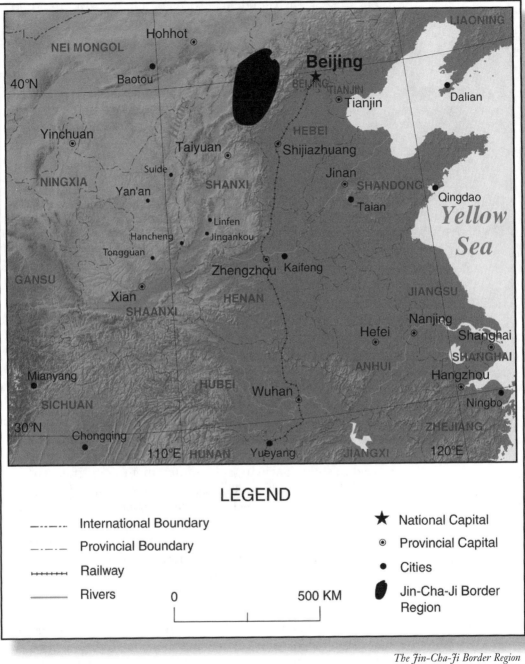

## LEGEND

| | |
|---|---|
| ------- International Boundary | ★ National Capital |
| ------- Provincial Boundary | ⊙ Provincial Capital |
| ++++++ Railway | ● Cities |
| ——— Rivers | ⬛ Jin-Cha-Ji Border Region |

0        500 KM

*The Jin-Cha-Ji Border Region was one of two areas in northern China controlled by the Communists*

*Yan'an, March 1938*

their guide had to keep jumping from the train along with the other passengers to run for cover in the fields. Luckily, on each occasion the Japanese failed to attack.

At Tongguan they changed trains and headed north for Linfen, where they were to meet an official of the Eighth Route Army. Minutes after their arrival, an air raid began. With neither anti-aircraft guns nor Chinese fighter planes to oppose them, Japanese planes cruised freely above the city dropping load after load of bombs. Following the guide, Bethune and Ewen gingerly picked their way through the shattered streets. Stepping around fallen debris and having to dodge groups of terrified people rushing for shelter, they found the appointed meeting place. But no one was there. With Japanese bombs falling only a few blocks away, they waited nervously while the guide rushed off to try to locate their contact. In less than a minute, he ran back to tell them that they would have to leave immediately. He had just learned from some fleeing soldiers that Japanese army units had already reached the city outskirts and were moving in their direction.

Back at the railway station they found total confusion. Both soldiers and civilians had surrounded the passenger train and were struggling to climb the steps to the coaches. Others were scaling ladders to reach the roofs. Bethune, Ewen and the guide found themselves trapped in the surging throng. Ewen tried to shout, gave up, and pointed to a freight train on a second track. Bethune signalled agreement with his hand and, by shoving, they were slowly able to snake their way through the terrified mob. Still clutching their baggage, they followed a handful of soldiers heading toward the train. Crossing the tracks, they climbed into an open freight car and fell exhausted on sacks of rice just as the train began to pull out of the station. Safe for the moment, they fell asleep as the train moved along on the return journey to Tongguan.

After several hours, Bethune woke. Realizing that the train had stopped, he called Ewen and they joined the soldiers, clambering over the sacks of rice and jumping to the ground. Finally they learned that the engineer had refused to go any farther. A slow-moving train was an ideal target for Japanese planes. In the middle of the night he had stopped long enough to disconnect his engine from the freight cars, leaving them on a siding.

There seemed to be little choice. Accepting the guide's advice, Bethune and Ewen decided to link up with the band of soldiers. But the soldiers refused to leave without the valuable cargo of rice on the train. Despite the fear of Japanese attack, the commanding officer walked to a nearby town where he was able to barter some of the rice for mules and carts. The following day, Bethune and Ewen joined the soldiers and a forty-two-cart mule train carrying four hundred bags of rice.

After only a few kilometres, they became the target for two Japanese planes. Running wildly in search of shelter, they were nearly deafened by the thunderous roar of the planes that dove to a height of less than sixty metres above them before dropping their bombs. Then the bombers climbed again, circled, and plummeted earthward, unloading the rest of their cargo of death. When the attack ended, eighteen of the pack mules were dead. The Chinese redistributed the sacks of rice and continued on their way.

On the banks of the Fen River, Bethune and Ewen tended the ailments of local peasants who discovered that a foreign doctor had arrived. All along the route they would stop to bind a wound, or to administer first aid to some of the needy among the swelling troop of refugees. On several occasions, with Ewen interpreting, Bethune exchanged angry words with the caravan leader, who had warned him that his delays were wasting valuable time. Word had reached them that a Japanese cavalry unit was less than forty kilometres away, heading, as they were, toward the Yellow River.

*On the banks of a Chinese river with guards of the Eighth Route Army*

Their little group of refugees crossed the river just ahead of the pursuing Japanese. But others, a few kilometres behind them, were not so lucky. After putting their belongings in a cave, Bethune and Ewen returned to the riverbank. Out on the water they saw two boats filled with refugees heading toward them in a desperate bid to escape from their pursuers. From the opposite side, Japanese machine-guns suddenly opened up, spraying their deadly fire into the slow-moving boats. As they watched in horror, the piercing screams of the helpless victims mingling with the sound of the answering Chinese guns assaulted their ears.

The following day they continued their trek, this time on foot. In the city of Hancheng they reported to a military base. Assured by the commander that he would notify Eighth Route Army officials in the city of Xi'an of their arrival, Bethune demanded to be put to work. For more than a week while they waited for transportation to Xi'an, they spent long hours treating wounded and diseased soldiers in the base hospital.

At last, after an arduous three-day trip south, they reached Xi'an. As Bethune and Ewen sat in the Eighth Route Army office, sipping the traditional cup of tea offered to guests, the soldiers congratulated them on their ability to come back from the dead. To Bethune's great amusement, they learned that foreign journalists in Wuhan had reported that the two Canadians were missing and believed killed by the Japanese when they had destroyed Linfen.

Though far from dead, they were exhausted. The date of their arrival in Xi'an was March 22, exactly one month from the day they had started on their journey. As a result, they were more than grateful for the treats their hosts had prepared for them. At a small hotel, each was given a room with a private bathroom. For both it was the first bath since leaving Wuhan. Then they were taken to a restaurant that served European food. Finally, they returned to their rooms to enjoy the ultimate luxury: a blissful sleep between white sheets on a bed with a mattress.

Welcome news awaited them the following morning. The Eighth Route Army had arranged for delivery of the medical supplies they had brought to China and stored in Hong Kong. They were to arrive with a Canadian missionary, Dr. Richard Brown, who had volunteered to spend part of his leave from his Anglican mission with Bethune and Ewen.

Their stay in Xi'an was brief because Bethune was impatient to push on and begin the task that had brought him to China. At his nagging insistence, the trucks carrying him, Ewen and some supplies began the tortuous three-day drive north to Yan'an, the Communist headquarters.

In the early evening of the last day of March, they saw the dim outline of the Yan'an pagoda on the highest hill above the valley that enclosed the Communist stronghold. As they descended the final stretch of winding road, they glimpsed lights from cave dwellings twinkling like fireflies in the surrounding hills.

When the driver pulled to a halt, Bethune hastily pushed open the door and jumped to the ground. Though tired and covered with dust, he was in high spirits. He almost knocked over someone standing beside the truck, one hand holding a bicycle, the other outstretched in greeting. In the gathering darkness he was unable to make out the face, but the stranger was obviously not Chinese.

"Welcome to Yan'an! My name is Hatem." As Bethune stepped closer to grasp the hand, he saw a short, strongly built man in the uniform of the Eighth Route Army. "You two must be tired after that hellish drive," he said. "After you get settled, I'll take you out for a night on the town—noodles at our cooperative restaurant, followed by a rare treat, courtesy of our charming enemy."

This was George Hatem, an American who had joined Mao Zedong's forces just after their arrival in Yan'an. Known by the Chinese as Dr. Ma, he was one of the very few qualified medical doctors in the Eighth Route Army.

After dinner they walked to Hatem's cave, where they discovered that the treat was coffee, captured from the Japanese.

*Mao Zedong*

For several hours Bethune peppered Hatem with questions. What kind of medical equipment did they have? How far from the front were they? How strong were the Japanese? At midnight after hours of intense talk, Bethune and Ewen said good night to an exhausted Dr. Hatem and returned to their rooms.

Bethune had just closed his door when a messenger appeared to announce that Chairman Mao wished to see him. Bethune called Ewen and followed the soldier, who led them to another cave. As they stepped inside the round-roofed dwelling, a tall, slender man dressed in the simple, blue cotton uniform of an ordinary soldier stepped forward with both hands outstretched. As his hands gripped Bethune's, Mao said, "*Huanying, huanying* (Welcome, welcome)."

Smiling warmly at the Chinese leader, Bethune returned the greeting in English. It was an emotional meeting and, Bethune knew, a rare one. Few foreigners had ever met this son of a Hunanese peasant who had become Chairman of the Chinese Communist Party.

Mao motioned Bethune and Ewen to chairs and pulled his closer to the pair. The other person in the room, Mao's interpreter, pointed to a bowl of peanuts, the only food they were able to offer their guests.

After hearing the story of their journey, Mao began to ask questions. What was the situation in Spain? Would the Western nations allow Japan to conquer China? Would England and France stand up to continued German and Italian aggression in Europe? Bethune offered his opinions, and then started to discuss his role in Yan'an. Mao explained that there was little medical equipment and few trained doctors and nurses in Yan'an. At the front, several hundred kilometres to the north, there were even fewer.

The four talked on until dawn, but when Bethune returned to his room, his mind refused to slow down. Unable to sleep, he paced back and forth, trying to figure out how he might be able to make a substantial contribution to the Chinese cause.

Within hours, his mood swung sharply in the opposite direction. Later that day he visited the military hospital. What he saw disgusted him. Conditions were appalling. Wards were caves cut out of the hills. On damp floors patients without sheets burrowed in filthy, lice-ridden straw mats that served as beds. In the rainy season, he learned, the outside path connecting the caves became a gushing torrent. At first Bethune reacted as he usually did when he was angry. Refusing to work under these conditions, he exploded in fury: "Good God, do they know nothing about simple sanitary measures? Their infection rate must break all known records." He was unprepared for what he saw and it was several days before he realized that, like it or not, his anger would not change conditions. He began to work in the hospital.

*With Dr. Richard Brown, who guided Bethune to Yan'an and Chinese general He Long.*

For nearly a month, he continuously demanded to be taken to the front. At first, the Chinese feared that he was too old, and refused. But Bethune's persistence, and his explanation that his Spanish experience had taught him that doctors had to go to the wounded, gradually wore them down. At last, the Chinese gave in.

After Dr. Brown arrived with the original medical supplies brought from Canada, Bethune sent Ewen back to Xi'an to buy more. Unwilling to wait for her return, Bethune and Brown, their truck filled with medicine, equipment and twelve soldiers, left Yan'an for the Jin-Cha-Ji Border Region. It was May 2, 1938.

# Chapter 6
# Jin-Cha-Ji

The first sun-filled days of their journey went well. Despite the rough surface of the narrow dirt track they followed, it was dry and the truck moved forward rather quickly. It took them through crusty loess hills formed by wind-borne soil deposited over the centuries. Set in irregular patterns and deeply furrowed by rain and wind, the strangely shaped, reddish-brown hills looked from a distance like huge, grooved chocolates.

Then the weather changed, and so did their pace. Steady, beating rain turned the dirt surface into a slippery, mucky goo that sharply slowed them down. Near the town of Suide, when the truck spluttered to a halt, Bethune jumped from the vehicle and, up to his ankles in the yellow mud, began to push. The Chinese were stunned. Never had they seen a foreigner do work that Chinese were usually forced to do. It was only the first of many signs that Bethune was obviously not an ordinary foreigner.

Beyond Suide the road ended suddenly and they had to continue by mule train. Now entering a more rugged, rocky mountain area, they often found themselves on slippery, threadlike paths with room for only one person to pass safely.

At each town along the route they stopped to treat soldiers and also civilians. Near the Yellow River at Gaojiachuan, they remained more than two weeks at a rear base hospital, where the two Canadian doctors were kept busy operating on the severely wounded. Frequent stops to treat the sick and wounded, and the arduous travelling conditions made the journey longer than they had expected. Near the beginning of June, they set foot on their last lap to the front.

In the late afternoon of June 17, they reached Jingangkou, headquarters of the Border Region in the Wu Tai Mountains. As they entered the town, they found soldiers and townspeople lining both sides of the main street waving and cheering. At the head of the welcoming committee was General Nieh Rongzhen, Commander-in-Chief of the Jin-Cha-Ji Border Region. After shaking hands, Nieh offered to lead Bethune to his quarters to rest before dinner.

*Bethune meeting General Nieh Rongzhen*

"Dinner? I don't want dinner. I've come here to treat the wounded, not to eat! Where are they?" was Bethune's sharp reply. Dr. Brown, interpreting for Bethune, tried to remove some of the sting from the angry words, but Bethune's mood was obvious to Nieh. Taken aback, the Chinese commander explained that Jingangkou was the military headquarters. The hospital was a day's ride away. Bethune eventually cooled off and agreed to spend the night before moving on, but Nieh quickly learned, as others had at Suide, that this foreigner was different.

As they rode on horseback to Songyankou the following day, Nieh explained the military situation. The Border Region of Jin-Cha-Ji was one of two areas in northern China controlled by the Communists. Within Jin-Cha-Ji there were more than thirteen million persons living in villages and towns scattered throughout the wild Wu Tai Mountains and on the broad Hebei plains. The enemy, based in Beijing, were rich in modern military equipment. Their planes dominated the skies and their tanks and trucks the roads. Their well-trained troops, equipped with superb rifles and machine-guns, suffered from no shortage of ammunition.

In contrast, the Eighth Route Army was made up of men, women, and children who lived in the area. Their strategy was to strike swiftly, attack small enemy groups, and disappear into the hills to become invisible among the peasant villages, where they waited for orders to attack again. They had had some success against the enemy, but they faced obstacles. Communications were poor, and often they were forced to rely on captured equipment. Above all, the soldiers feared being wounded, for to be wounded in guerrilla war often meant death. Unlike the Japanese troops who were served by an efficient medical corps, Chinese guerrilla units were lucky to receive more than primitive first aid treatment for their wounds.

Bethune gradually began to realize the scope of his work and a plan took shape in his mind. His first task was to treat the wounded in Songyankou, the major base hospital in Jin-Cha-Ji. This "hospital" consisted of patients on straw mats in peasant huts scattered through the town. There were neither sheets nor electricity, little medicine and few instruments. Bethune had more instruments than the entire Eighth Route Army. Moreover, he had already used most of the medicines he had brought tending the wounded en route to Jin-Cha-Ji.

He would have to begin from scratch, working under conditions that he did not yet fully understand. He and Brown spent the first several days moving from hut to hut examining and classifying the wounded. Next, they worked steadily for almost a month operating on the worst cases. Every afternoon they gave lectures to the medical personnel. Few of the Chinese had received any formal training and none had graduated from a medical or nursing school. Every week Bethune and Brown brought all medical workers together for staff meetings. An organization was taking shape.

In his few free moments Bethune was forced to invent and manufacture many of the instruments he needed. Here, in the mountains, he had to work without technicians and the unending supply of material that had been available in Montreal. He built an operating room in an old, unused temple. He designed and constructed leg and arm splints, a sterilizer and stretcher racks.

By mid-July, Dr. Brown's leave had ended and he returned to his mission. Shortly after their arrival in Jin-Cha-Ji, Bethune had sent a letter to Yan'an to Jean Ewen to tell her not to follow him when she returned from Xi'an. Conditions in the Border Region, he explained, were too rugged.

Now he was alone, the only doctor for hundreds of kilometres, with a potential patient list of more than one hundred and fifty thousand guerrilla soldiers. Instead of frightening Bethune, this awesome responsibility inspired him. He prepared a list of priorities. First, he needed a hospital that would serve two purposes: a treatment centre for the wounded and a training school for the doctors and nurses that he would have to

*Instruction on the battlefield. Notice that students are taking notes.*

teach. Secondly, he would write teaching manuals and have them translated. Thirdly, as soon as possible, he would go on an inspection tour of the entire Border Region to learn the condition of medical services.

He approached General Nieh with his proposal for a hospital and found him doubtful. Nieh carefully explained that nothing in a guerrilla war could be considered permanent. If the Japanese advanced into the area, the hospital would be destroyed and time and money would be wasted. Bethune listened impatiently, paused, and stubbornly repeated his demands. At last, Nieh agreed to consult the Military Council in Yan'an.

Much against their better judgment and partly to please Bethune because of his sincere devotion to his work, they agreed to a hospital in Songyankou. The news thrilled Bethune who had long ago chosen the site, an unused Buddhist temple partially hidden by a grove of trees high up above the road entering the town. He had also worked out in his mind plans for the hospital's design and construction.

Work began the moment Bethune learned of the Military Council's decision. With Bethune shouting directions, the entire village was mobilized in the cooperative effort. While men and boys lugged stones and carried lumber up the hill, women sewed blankets and sheets and pieced together mattresses. In less than two months, a thirty-six-bed infirmary had been put together in the remote village. The workers and soldiers proudly named it the Model Hospital.

Somehow, between time spent helping build the hospital and operating on the wounded, Bethune was able to complete a medical textbook for the course he was preparing to give starting in mid-October. But both book and course had to be delayed. A few days after the opening ceremonies of the Model Hospital on September 15, 1938, the Japanese began a major offensive in Hebei province. When Bethune convinced Nieh that he was needed at the front, he hastily assembled and led a ten-man mobile unit to the battle zone. The offensive had spoiled his plans for training doctors, but before leaving he told Nieh, "The best way is to go with these people and instruct them in the field under actual conditions."

It was several weeks before he found out how thoroughly his plans had been destroyed. A few days after the mobile unit had left Songyankou, Japanese troops entered the area,

*Opening of the Model Hospital*

attacked the village and demolished the Model Hospital. When the news reached Bethune on the march, he was heartbroken. Only then did he begin to understand the value of Nieh's warning that nothing could be permanent in a guerrilla war. He had learned a valuable lesson the hard way.

But there was no time for regret. The heavy November snow did little to slow down the steady Japanese advance. Day after day, Bethune's unit gingerly made its way along icy mountain trails to reach the wounded. Near the end of November, the Chinese began to counterattack. Warned in advance, Bethune's unit arrived in the mountain village of Heisi and set up an operating room in a small temple. Their only defences against the sub-zero temperature were a few slender cypress trees surrounding the temple, a sheet for a roof, and a roaring fire around which they huddled waiting for the wounded.

The first casualties arrived on stretchers in the late afternoon. Bethune and his two assistants began to work. Soon they were far behind, as the temple filled with wounded soldiers. Taking brief naps, the three men continued throughout the night and the following day. Only during the second night, when two other doctors arrived, did Bethune and his assistants stop for a few hours sleep. After this brief break, Bethune continued to operate until the following morning. In forty hours the unit had treated seventy-one wounded soldiers.

It was a magnificent effort, but what impressed Bethune most were the results. By being so close to the battle, he was able to operate before there had been much loss of blood or time for infection to set in. At least one-third of the wounded would be able to fight the Japanese again within a month. He had applied his Spanish experience under Chinese conditions. He wrote to Nieh:

> *We have demonstrated to our own satisfaction and I hope to the satisfaction of the Army commanders the value of this type of treatment of wounds. The time is past and gone in which doctors will wait for patients to come to them. Doctors must go to the wounded and the earlier the better.*

This was a turning point for Bethune. He now realized that the mobile medical unit, fully equipped and manned by trained medical personnel, could be of tremendous value in the saving of lives. He had not given up his plan for a permanent hospital, but he understood that the time to build it was only when the Japanese had been driven out of the area.

After Heisi, the Japanese winter offensive ended and both sides welcomed the breathing space. It gave Bethune the chance to open a new headquarters in the town of Yangjiazhuang where he began to plan the formation of a number of mobile medical units.

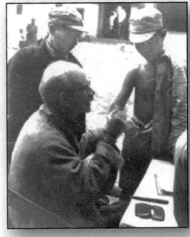

*Bethune treating a young soldier*

As the New Year dawned, he looked back to the beginning of this great adventure. It must have seemed so long ago. Now he was Medical Advisor to the Eighth Route Army and already a legendary figure. Stories of the tireless work and devotion of "Bai Qiuen," as he was known to the Chinese, spread among the troops throughout the Border Region. One told how, on the trip to Jin-Cha-Ji, he had come with a suitcase of foreign clothes which he gave away to patients he had tended in the little villages. Another emphasized that he showed as much concern for civilians as he did for soldiers. As he was passing through a village, he noticed a child with a harelip. Signalling the unit to halt, he jumped from his horse and asked his interpreter to explain to the child's mother that a simple operation would allow her daughter to speak normally. The surprised mother welcomed Bethune, who quickly performed the operation and continued on the march.

*Bethune operating in China, 1939*

As months passed, he was constantly on the move, sleeping in peasant huts, eating the simple food and sharing the hardships of the people he treated. Despite these conditions, in August he wrote in his diary:

*I have operated all day and am tired. Ten cases, 5 of them very serious . . . It is true I am tired but I don't think I have been so happy for a long time. I am content. I am doing what I want to do.*

Yet, by January, 1939, he was beginning to admit to weariness and homesickness. He wrote to a Canadian friend:

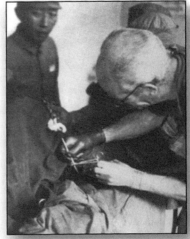

*When he was not operating or teaching, he was writing text-books, reports to General Nieh, or letters to North America pleading for financial aid*

*My life is pretty rough and sometimes tough as well. It reminds me of my early days up in the Northern bush. The village is like all other Chinese villages, made of mud and stone, one-storey houses, in groups (families) of compounds. Three or four houses are enclosed in a compound facing each other. In the compound are the pigs, dogs, donkeys, etc. Everything is filthy—the people, their houses, etc. I have one house to myself. It has a brick oven running along the single room. In this I have my cot and table. I have made myself a tin stove in which is burnt coal and wood. The windows (one) are papered with white paper. The floor is packed mud, so are the walls...Let me confess that on the 1st of the New Year I had an attack of homesickness! Memories of New York, Montreal and Toronto! If I were not so busy I could find reasons enough for a holiday. With the kindest remembrances of you all . . .*

Letters like this were few, for he was far too involved in his work. Early in the new year, medical personnel from each district of the Border Region arrived in Yangjiazhuang to take an intensive medical course. In three weeks, Bethune taught each of the thirty men and women the functions and responsibilities of a doctor, nurse and nurse's assistant that he expected them to practise on the battlefield. These students later returned to their areas to pass on their knowledge.

He was now ready to begin his delayed inspection tour of the Border Region. Sitting proudly astride a white horse captured from the Japanese and presented to him by General Nieh, he led his eighteen-member mobile unit to the Hebei plain. Because the area was occupied by the Japanese, they frequently had to ride at night to cross Japanese lines.

*Leading his mobile medical group on horseback*

On one occasion, just as they were leaving a village, a Japanese cavalry patrol spotted them. Someone shouted and a shot rang out. Bethune spurred his horse forward and the unit followed, with the Japanese in pursuit. Burdened by their medical equipment, they were slower than the Japanese who were narrowing the gap to firing range. Suddenly they saw coming toward them one of their own patrols rounding a bend less than a kilometre away. Almost at the same time, the Japanese noticed the enemy patrol and, firing a few useless rounds of bullets, turned abruptly and headed back. It was a narrow escape in a war that was exposing him to far more danger than he had known in Spain.

Continuing onward, they visited village hospitals scattered over the broad Hebei plain. They went from hospital to hospital, calling staff meetings, touring wards and making suggestions. Usually Bethune remained for several days operating on the most severely wounded, watched by eager young eyes that noted his every move. He had become a travelling teacher.

When blood was needed, he sometimes gave his own, despite the opposition of his assistants. In a village where he had used his own blood to transfuse a wounded soldier, the word passed among the amazed peasants who gathered in curiosity outside the hut where he was operating. Aware that they were afraid of giving their own blood, Bethune carefully explained through his interpreter how vital the donation was in saving lives, and that the donor would feel no pain. When he asked for volunteers, a frightened, but brave young man meekly emerged from the group and offered himself. Lying on his back on a door that Bethune had been using as an operating table, he closed his eyes, squeezed his fists tightly and turned his head to the side. Bethune then inserted a syringe in the boy's arm and withdrew a few cubic centimetres of blood, which he showed to the awestruck crowd. When the painless removal of blood had been completed, the smiling boy got up and stood at the side of Bethune proudly flexing his arm. Bethune quickly took the opportunity to urge the villagers to have their blood typed and written on a piece of cloth sewn to their clothing. The demonstration was effective. One by one, villagers moved closer to Bethune, their bare arms extended. This became known as "the living blood bank."

The tour had gone well and there had been little fighting until the end of April. On April 26, the unit was called to a savage battle near the town of Qihui. Stationing themselves in a temple only five kilometres from the fighting, they were setting up their operating room when the wounded began to arrive. Bethune worked like a demon ignoring the shells that were falling near them. Even when one crashed through the wall, scattering stone and debris over the floor, his assistants could

*Ho Zixin was assigned to look after Bethune*

not convince him to leave. After several hours, a doctor was finally able to persuade him to rest. He agreed, walked over to a container of icy water and briefly immersed his head in it. Then he walked around the room, stretched, and sat down for ten minutes before returning to work.

Under pressure from his assistants, he repeated this process from time to time until the battle ended. In his report to General Nieh, written several days later, he minimized his and the unit's achievement—one hundred and fifteen operations in sixty-nine consecutive hours. But the soldiers and people of the Border Region soon learned of Bethune's extraordinary performance at Qihui. Within days the story had spread throughout the mountains and over the plains, acting as a powerful morale-booster to soldiers of the Eighth Route Army.

Bethune continued with the unit into the late spring, racing from battle to battle, setting up equipment never more than five kilometres from the front. When he returned to his headquarters in July, he laid plans for the formation of seven more mobile units before the end of the year.

He had not given up his idea of a permanent medical school and he decided to spend part of the summer directing the construction of the replacement for the Model Hospital. For this he chose a new site, the village of Niuyankou, which was far from the Japanese lines. Even before the new hospital school opened its doors on September 18, 1939, he had already begun to teach his students. The text they were using was his *Organization and Techniques for Divisional Mobile Operating Units* that he had finished near the end of the summer.

In his teaching he always emphasized that a good doctor combined the skills of four craftsmen: blacksmith, carpenter, tailor and barber. He had worked with blacksmiths shaping iron splints, and with carpenters building his collapsible operating table. He had designed and sewn saddlebags and shown his students how to shave a patient before a brain operation. His own inventive ability constantly amazed the Chinese. One of his most useful creations was a wooden case that fitted on the back of a mule. Containing medicines and supplies for a hundred operations, five hundred dressings and five hundred prescriptions, it could be readied for an operation in less than thirty minutes.

His decision to build the new teaching hospital resulted from his analysis of what he had done since he had left Yan'an fifteen months earlier. He knew his value to the Chinese. He had been a battle surgeon, inventor, author and teacher, but his greatest contribution was the last. The Chinese learned quickly and well. They lacked only money to purchase the necessary supplies.

Time and time again he wrote to friends in Canada and the United States pleading for money. In one letter he wrote:

*What is the China Aid Council doing for China, for the 8th Route Army? How much money have they sent? Are they sending more doctors or technicians? Am I to have assistance? Am I to have the medical supplies I have been asking for for 5 months? I have exactly 27 tubes of catgut left and ½ lb. of carbolic acid. I have one knife and 6 artery forceps—all the rest I have distributed. There remains 2½ lbs of chloroform. After that is finished we will operate without anaesthetics. Now for Marx' sake, get busy!*

But his pleas went unheeded. In August he decided to return to Canada to go on another tour to raise funds.

He also knew that he was rapidly losing strength. In August he wrote to an American friend:

*My health is pretty fair—teeth need attention, one ear has been completely deaf for 3 months, glasses for eyes need correction, but apart from these minor things and being pretty thin, I'm OK.*

Perhaps he was trying to convince himself that the long winter marches through the snow-filled mountains, the scanty diet of millet, eggs and tea, and the shattering tension of operating to the constant echo of gunfire, had had little effect upon him. The truth was that he had aged twenty years within fifteen months. He was gaunt, weak and fragile.

He was at least willing to admit to homesickness.

*I dream of coffee, of rare roast beef, of apple pie and ice cream. Mirages of heavenly food. Books—are books still being written? Is music still being played? Do you dance, drink beer, look at pictures? What do clean white sheets in a soft bed feel like? Do women still love to be loved?*

Bethune planned to leave for home in October, but not before completing a short inspection tour of his hospitals. On the last lap of the tour, a surprise Japanese advance forced him to rush his unit to Modian Mountain.

On October 28 he cut his finger during an operation, had it bandaged and finished his work. A few days later he was performing a brain operation on a soldier. The area he had to deal with was highly infected. Because his immune system was weak, his cut had not healed well and remained partially open. He was not wearing gloves—there weren't any.

Three days later he complained of being tired and noticed that his finger had swollen. Soon he was feverish and an abscess had formed in his armpit. He had contracted septicaemia (blood-poisoning).

On November 11 he wrote to Lang' Lin, his interpreter:

*I came back from the front yesterday. There was no good in my being there. I couldn't get out of bed or operate. . . Had uncontrolled chills and fever all day. Temp. around 39.6 C, bad. . . Next day (9th) more vomiting all day, high fever. Next day (10th) regiment commander (3rd Regiment) instructed I be sent back, useless for work. Vomiting on stretcher all the day. High fever, over 40 C. I think I have either septicaemia from the gangrenous finger or typhus fever. Can't get to sleep, mentally very bright. Phenacitin and aspirin, woven's powder, antipyrin, caffeine, all useless. . .*
*I feel freely today. Pain over heart. . . Will see you tomorrow, I expect.*

*Unable to find a Union Jack, the Chinese draped an American flag behind Bethune's body*

He knew that he would never see the dawn. As he lay on a cot in a peasant hut in the mountain village of Huangshikou, one of the doctors he had trained pleaded with him to allow him to amputate his arm. Slowly shaking his head, Bethune murmured, "No use. I am going to die."

Throughout the night the nurses and doctors stood around his bed, quietly and unashamedly crying. From time to time, they would replace a cold compress on his forehead. At last, his determined resistance broke down and his breathing stopped. It was twenty minutes past five on the morning of November 12, 1939.

# Chapter 7
# Shijiazhuang

Bethune's death was a severe loss to the Eighth Route Army. Many had come to know and respect this temperamental, high-spirited and brilliant man. Soldiers in the field who had never seen him, but who had heard the stories of his dedication and self-sacrifice, had chanted slogans before going into battle, such as, "We fight at the front. If we are wounded, we have Bai Qiuen to treat us. Attack!" From his personal guard, his interpreter, the doctors and nurses he had worked with and the wounded soldiers he had treated, down to the girl whose harelip he had cured—all would remember him. When Mao Zedong learned of Bethune's death, he wrote a moving eulogy called *In Memory of Norman Bethune*.

The people in the Wu Tai mountains built a memorial tomb which the Japanese later used for machine-gun practice. When the enemy had been driven out, the determined Chinese rebuilt the tomb.

After the war, they moved the grave to the city of Shijiazhuang and placed beside it a larger-than-life statue of Bethune in the most prominent position in the Park of the Martyrs' Tombs of the Military Region of North China. The memorial park is a tribute to more than twenty-five thousand Chinese who died fighting the Japanese and the Guomindang, yet the tomb of Norman Bethune, a Canadian, is its major attraction. Near the tomb and statue, they later built a large pavilion in his honour.

Across the road is the Norman Bethune International Peace Hospital, and beside it is a museum that tells his life

*One of the many heroic statues of Bethune in China*

*Chinese stamps honouring Bethune*

story in photographs and line drawings. In the centre of the building is a glass case holding his few personal possessions that survived the war: a typewriter, some instruments and papers. At the entrance to the hospital stands a statue of Bethune that looks down the road leading to the main door. Each year hundreds of thousands of Chinese and foreigners visit Shijiazhuang to pay homage to Bethune.

After the Communists came to power in China in 1949, Chinese outside the Border Region began to hear the story of Bai Qiuen. The story of his life was taught in the schools. Two postage stamps were issued bearing his image. Posters, statuettes, magazines and books reminded the Chinese of his contribution to their struggle. Then, during the Great Proletarian Cultural Revolution in the late 1960s, *In Memory of Norman Bethune* was made required reading in all schools. Not only was every student expected to read Mao's essay, but many of them, as well as millions of adults, learned to recite it from memory. The Chinese were taught that Bethune had the personal qualities of dedication and self-sacrifice, and willingness to help others that Mao and other leaders claimed they wanted their people to imitate. Today in China, years after the death of Mao Zedong and the rejection of almost all the values of the Cultural Revolution, Norman Bethune, the only Canadian name known to most Chinese, still commands deep respect.

# Chapter 8
# Canada: The Legend

Although Bethune became a martyr in China, his name remained little known in Canada. The reason was political. Throughout the Cold War that began in the late 1940s, most Canadians remained hostile to communism. When the communists came to power in China, Canada did not recognize them as the legitimate government of that country, and for more than twenty years, the two nations refused to deal with one another.

During this period, there were attempts in Canada to draw attention to Bethune's life story. A biography, *The Scalpel, The Sword*, appeared in 1952, and twelve years later, the National Film Board of Canada produced a documentary film, *Bethune*. But when the book and the film won praise in several communist countries, there was resentment in Canada. Few Canadians were attracted to someone who was a hero to communists.

Though many Canadians remained hostile to communism, Prime Minister Pierre Elliott Trudeau's government decided in 1970 to establish diplomatic relations with China. This change in policy had a marked affect on Bethune's reputation in Canada. In a move designed to please the Chinese, and also to help Canadian businessmen gain entry into the huge Chinese trade market, the Trudeau government named Bethune "a Canadian of national historic significance." It then bought the house in Gravenhurst, Ontario, where Bethune had been born, and had it restored to the structure and appearance it had had at his birth. In 1976 the Bethune Memorial House was opened to the public.

Bethune's suddenly acquired respectability triggered an interest in him that spiraled into a kind of "Bethunemania." Various writers, poets, playwrights, artists and movie producers became fascinated with the man and his achievements. And so began a parade of tributes that continues today. It started with a new biography, *Bethune*, and a collection of his writings and photographs of him, entitled *The Mind of Norman Bethune*; following these was a book of reminiscences by former colleagues called *Bethune The Montreal Years*, and a study of his art and writings, entitled *The Politics of Passion: Norman Bethune's Writing and Art*. Another biography, *Norman Bethune: a life of passionate conviction*, has recently appeared.

In addition, there have been numerous poems, several plays, and sculptures. Films have also been made. In 1977, the Canadian Broadcasting Corporation produced *Bethune*, a tele-film based on the biography of the same name. Playing the role of Bethune, the Canadian actor Donald Sutherland won an *Etrog*, the award given for the best performance by an actor in Canadian television. Thirteen years later, in the centenary of Bethune's birth, the film *Bethune: The Making of a Hero* was released. It also starred Donald Sutherland, who had for many years been an admirer of Bethune.

Schools and universities followed the trend. A Toronto high school, and a college at Toronto's York University were named after him.

Finally his own profession, medicine, granted him recognition. In 1998, the Canadian Medical Hall of Fame admitted Bethune to its list of men and women who have made valuable contributions to medical science in this country.

The most recent tribute has come from the people in the town where he was born. The mayor and councillors of Gravenhurst authorized the erection of a larger than life statue of Bethune in the centre of the town. In August, 2000, Her Excellency, Adrienne Clarkson, the governor-general of Canada, presided at the unveiling of the statue. And so, in this sense, one hundred and ten years after he was born, Norman Bethune came home.

But not all Canadians have been pleased by the growing interest in Bethune. Among them are those who despise his politics. Others point out that he was sometimes theatrical, brusque, and even arrogant.

It is easy to understand the criticism of his unusual, and sometimes apparently objectionable behaviour. On the other hand, the reason he appeared this way to some people can be explained by his persistent refusal to conceal his feelings when he disagreed with others. In every situation, whether personal, professional, or political, he always made his position clear. He was not a fence-sitter.

Norman Bethune was, above all, an individualist who had the courage, the gritty determination, and in some situations, the foolish obstinacy to tread the path his self-reliant and independent spirit led him to choose. In a letter to a friend, he wrote:

> *You must remember my father was an evangelist and I come of a race of men violent, unstable, of passionate convictions and wrong-headedness, intolerant yet with it all a vision of truth and a drive to carry them to it even though it leads, as it has done in my family, to their destruction.*

*Bethune at the Great Wall*

Controversy often paralyzes people, yet it seemed to attract and stimulate Norman Bethune. "I must learn," he once told Frances, "to stop shocking people." In death, no less than in life, that wish has never been fulfilled.

# Norman Bethune

| | |
|---|---|
| 1890 | Born on March 3 in Gravenhurst, Ontario |
| 1909 | Begins studies at University of Toronto |
| 1912 | Spends a year working at Frontier College |
| 1914 | Joins the Royal Canadian Army Medical Corps |
| 1915 | Wounded by shrapnel at Ypres |
| 1916 | Completes medical studies |
| 1917 | Enlists in the Royal Navy |
| 1919 | Begins internship at Hospital for Sick Children in London, England |
| 1923 | Marries Frances Campbell Penney |
| 1924 | Sets up medical practice in Detroit, Michigan |
| 1926 | Enters Trudeau Sanatorium in Saranac Lake, N.Y., with tuberculosis |
| 1927 | Frances divorces him |
| 1928 | Joins the staff at Royal Victoria Hospital in Montreal |
| 1929 | Remarries Frances (divorced again in 1933) |
| 1933 | Appointed Chief of Thoracic Surgery at Sacred Heart Hospital, Cartierville |
| 1935 | Attends scientific congress in the Soviet Union<br>Joins the Communist Party |
| 1936 | Goes to Spain with medical supplies and sets up blood transfusion unit |
| 1937 | Returns to Canada for speaking tour |
| 1938 | Sails for China to help the Communists under Mao Zedong<br>Sets up mobile medical units to operate close to battles |
| 1939 | Cuts his finger during an operation and gets blood-poisoning<br>Dies on November 12 |

## Further Reading

Allen, Ted and Gordon, Sydney. *The Scalpel, The Sword.* Toronto: McClelland and Stewart Limited, 1952.

Hannant, Larry. *The Politics of Passion: Norman Bethune's Writing and Art.* Toronto: University of Toronto Press, 1998.

MacLeod, Wendell; Park, Libbie; Ryerson, Stanley. *Bethune The Montreal Years.* Toronto: Lorimer, 1978.

Stewart, Roderick. *Bethune.* Toronto: New Press, 1973.

*The Mind of Norman Bethune.* Toronto: Fitzhenry & Whiteside, 2002.

Wilson, John. *Norman Bethune: a life of passionate conviction.* Montreal: XYZ Publishing, 1999.

## Credits

The publishers wish to acknowledge their gratitude to the following who have given permission to use copyrighted illustrations in this book:

Bethune Memorial House, pages 4, 6, 10, 11, 12, 15, 18, 19, 21, 23, 29, 31, 36, 40, 41, 44, 45, 50, 51, 52, 56, 57, 58

Canadian Parks Service, 24, 27, 31, 32, 33, 34, 36, 43, 52, 61

The National Film Board, pages 9 and 28

All other pictures are from the collection of the author.

## Index